MAY -- 2024

WITHDRAWN

WINNETKA-NORTHFIELD
PUBLIC LIBRARY DISTRICT
WINNETKA, IL 60093
847-446-7220

MYTHICAL CREATURES

FUSION

THE PHOENIX

by
Charis Mather

BEARPORT
PUBLISHING

Minneapolis, Minnesota

Credits

All images are courtesy of Shutterstock.com, unless otherwise specified. With thanks to Getty Images, Thinkstock Photo, and iStockphoto.

Recurring images – Yauhen Paleski, Gaidamashchuk, Rikley Stock, SpicyTruffel. Cover – happy_fox_art. 4–5 – Macrovector, Chittakon Khummun, masik0553, Sunti. 6–7 – Anastasiya_g. 8–9 – Babin, Knumina Studios. 10–11 – Cornelis Troost (Wikimedia Commons), Daniel VILLAFRUELA (Wikimedia Commons), ClassicVector, Declan Hillman, Hennadii H. 12–13 – argus, Gustave Moreau (Wikimedia Commons), WeihrauchWelt. 14–15 – Declan Hillman, etotishina, Ellerslie77. 16–17 – jaja, scubadesign, Wang LiQiang, 4zevar. 18–19 – houchi, JohnnyMellado (Wikimedia Commons). 20–21 – Mark Szallos-Farkas, michel arnault. 22–23 – Africa Studio, Samuel Borges Photography.

Bearport Publishing Company Product Development Team

President: Jen Jenson; Director of Product Development: Spencer Brinker; Managing Editor: Allison Juda; Associate Editor: Naomi Reich; Associate Editor: Tiana Tran; Senior Designer: Colin O'Dea; Associate Designer: Elena Klinkner; Associate Designer: Kayla Eggert; Product Development Assistant: Owen Hamlin

Library of Congress Cataloging-in-Publication Data

Names: Mather, Charis, 1999- author.
Title: The phoenix / by Charis Mather.
Description: Fusion Books. | Minneapolis, Minnesota : Bearport Publishing Company, [2024] | Series: Mythical creatures | "This edition is published by arrangement with BookLife Publishing"--Copyright page.
Identifiers: LCCN 2023031461 (print) | LCCN 2023031462 (ebook) | ISBN 9798889163046 (hardcover) | ISBN 9798889163091 (paperback) | ISBN 9798889163138 (ebook)
Subjects: LCSH: Phoenix (Mythical bird)--Juvenile literature.
Classification: LCC GR830.P4 M38 2024 (print) | LCC GR830.P4 (ebook) | DDC 398.24/54--dc23/eng/20230802
LC record available at https://lccn.loc.gov/2023031461
LC ebook record available at https://lccn.loc.gov/2023031462

© 2024 BookLife Publishing
This edition is published by arrangement with BookLife Publishing.

North American adaptations © 2024 Bearport Publishing Company. All rights reserved. No part of this publication may be reproduced in whole or in part, stored in any retrieval system, or transmitted in any form or by any means, electronic, mechanical, photocopying, recording, or otherwise, without written permission from the publisher.

For more information, write to Bearport Publishing, 5357 Penn Avenue South, Minneapolis, MN 55419.

CONTENTS

Myths, Magic, and More. 4

What Does the Phoenix Look Like? 6

The Halo 8

Reborn 10

This and That 12

Immortality 14

Where the Phoenix Lives 16

Mythical Look-Alikes 18

Real-Life Phoenixes? 20

Mysterious Mythical Creatures 22

Glossary 24

Index 24

MYTHS, MAGIC, AND MORE

Most people have heard of the flaming, magical bird known as the phoenix. But you probably haven't seen it in real life. Why not? Because the phoenix is a **mythical** creature!

For thousands of years, people from all over the world have told stories about the phoenix. Different **legends** talk about the creature in different ways. Let's learn what the stories have to say!

There are stories of the phoenix from Ancient Egypt, Greece, and Rome.

WHAT DOES THE PHOENIX LOOK LIKE?

Let's take a closer look at this flying beast.

Feathers

Phoenix feathers are colored like a burning flame. They come in reds, golds, or even purples.

Head

A small group of feathers, called a crest, stands on top of the bird's head.

Halo

A round, golden band of light circles the top of its head.

Beak

Like many birds, the phoenix has a curved beak.

Claws

Long, sharp claws are thought to help the phoenix hold and climb things.

THE HALO

Many stories about the phoenix say it has a halo. But where did the halo come from?

Legends say the halo around the bird's head glows bright. That might be because the phoenix is often connected with the sun in stories.

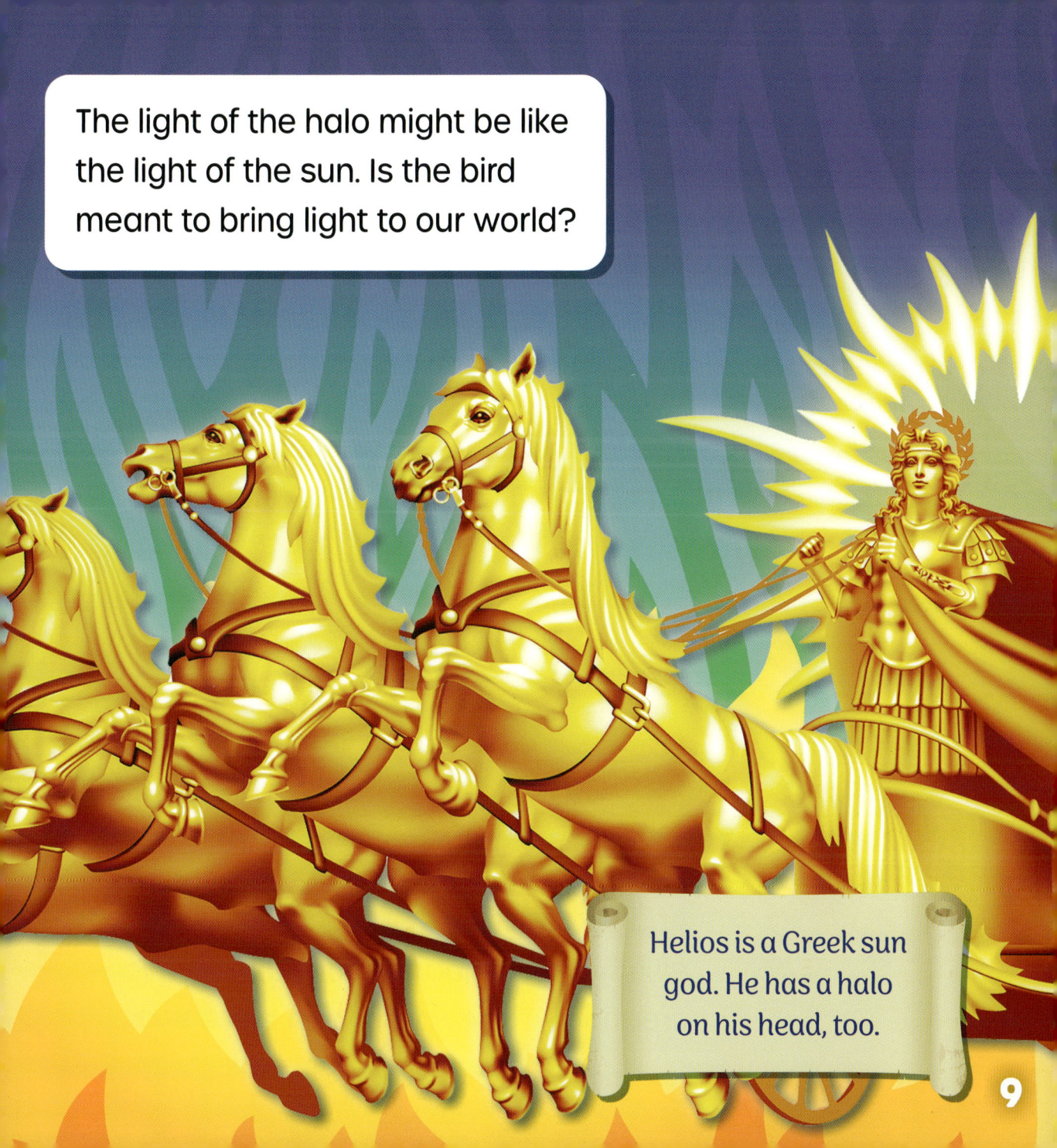

The light of the halo might be like the light of the sun. Is the bird meant to bring light to our world?

Helios is a Greek sun god. He has a halo on his head, too.

REBORN

Apart from stories of a golden halo, what else have we heard about this mythical creature? The phoenix can be **reborn**!

Stories say the phoenix can live for about 500 years. As it reaches the end of its life, the bird builds a nest. Then, the phoenix bursts into flames. A new phoenix rises from the **ashes**.

Could an animal really be reborn? Some people wonder if it could be possible.

THIS AND THAT

Legends say the phoenix would sing a beautiful song every morning. Many other birds sing as the sun comes up, too!

Most birds eat small insects and fruits. But the phoenix eats a gummy goo called frankincense (FRANG-kin-*sens*) that comes from certain trees.

Frankincense

Many people say frankincense smells woodsy and sweet.

People think of the phoenix as a **symbol** of being reborn. Some say butterflies have this meaning, too, because they come from caterpillars.

13

IMMORTALITY

Not all legends about the phoenix talk about death and rebirth. Others say the phoenix is a sign of **immortality**.

Some stories say there is only one phoenix. It lives forever.

14

In the past, some people used the bird as a symbol for their **empires**. They wanted their territories to last forever.

WHERE THE PHOENIX LIVES

Some stories say the phoenix lives in Arabia, which is an area in the Middle East. The bird stays near a cool well, where it bathes and sings.

Other stories say Egypt is the phoenix's home. They think it flew to the ancient city of Heliopolis after it was reborn. There, it went to live in a **temple**.

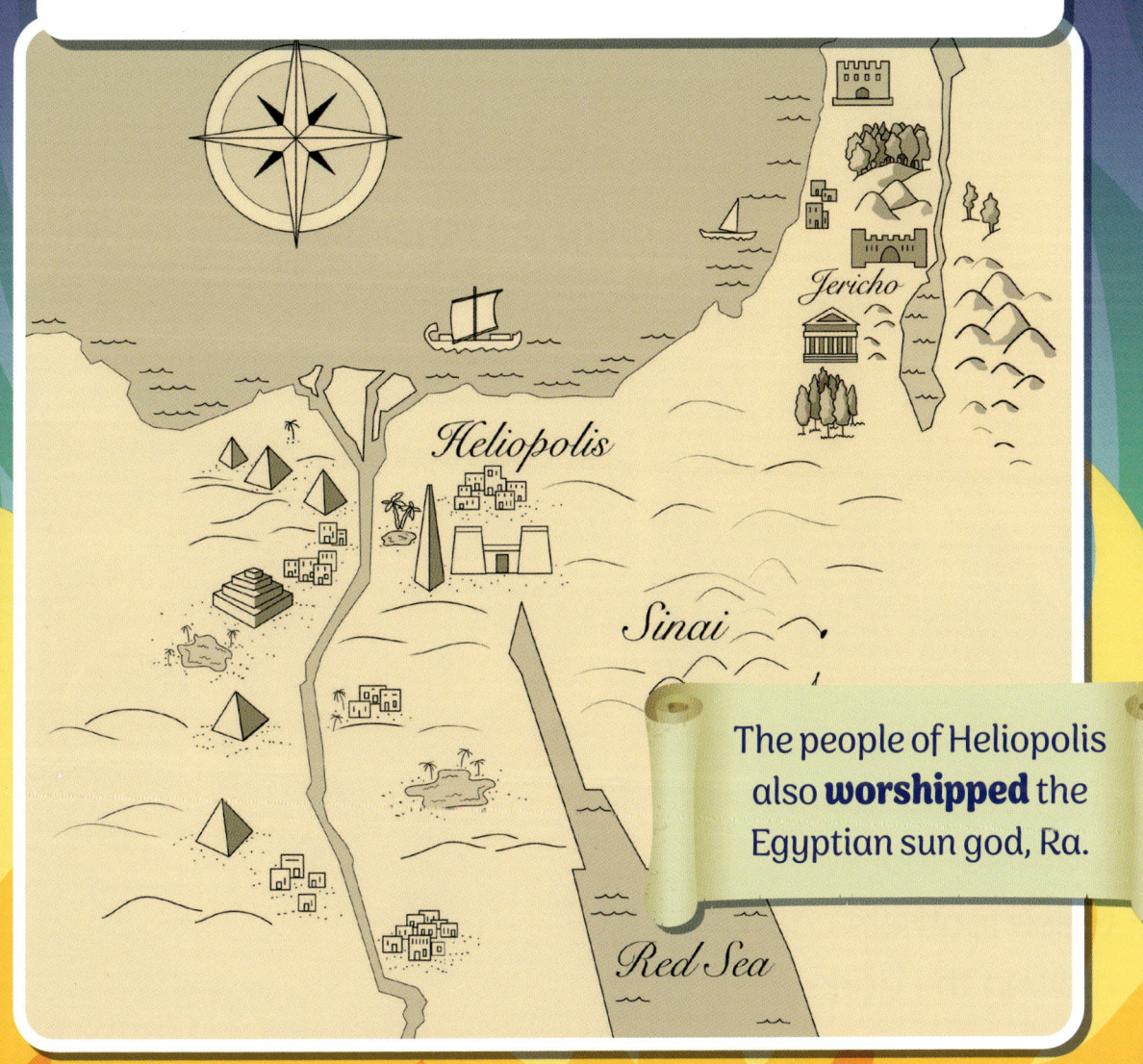

The people of Heliopolis also **worshipped** the Egyptian sun god, Ra.

MYTHICAL LOOK-ALIKES

There are other mythical creatures like the phoenix. Let's look at a few.

Firebirds have bright red and gold feathers, too. But these feathers can glow in the dark.

A firebird

The alicanto comes from Chilean legends. In the stories, this bird eats metals, which change the color of its feathers. If the alicanto eats a piece of gold, its feathers will turn a golden color!

The alicanto

REAL-LIFE PHOENIXES?

Where do stories about the phoenix come from? Maybe from real animals. . . .

Birds-of-Paradise

Birds-of-paradise live in tropical forests. Like the phoenix, their feathers are colored in reds and yellows.

Golden Pheasants

Also known as rainbow pheasants, golden pheasants are very colorful. They have long tail feathers the same color as phoenix feathers in legends.

Immortal Jellyfish

Immortal jellyfish do not die of old age. Instead, they can repeat their life cycle over and over again!

MYSTERIOUS MYTHICAL CREATURES

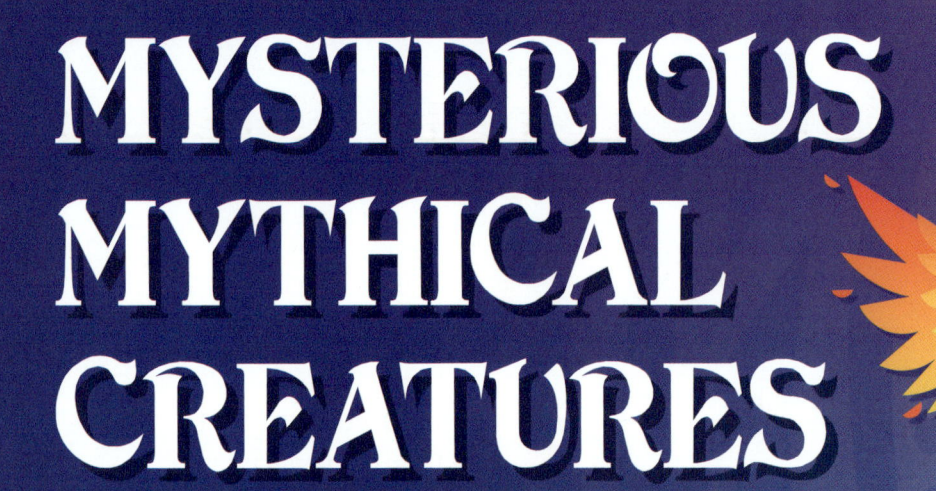

The phoenix is a fun, yet mysterious creature. We can learn a lot from stories about this fiery flying beast.

If you can't get enough of the phoenix, just read some books! There is so much to explore about this magical, mythical creature.

GLOSSARY

ashes the powder left behind after something burns

empires large areas, countries, or regions ruled by a single person

immortality the ability to live forever

legends stories from the past that may have a mix of truth and made-up things

mythical based on stories or something made up in the imagination

reborn born again

symbol a design or object that stands for something else

temple a building used for worship

worshipped shown great honor and respect

INDEX

Arabia 16
ashes 11
colors 6, 19–21
Egypt 5, 17
feathers 6–7, 18–21
god 9, 17
halo 7–10
Heliopolis 17
lights 7, 9, 18
nests 11
songs 12
sun 8–9, 12, 17